# STAND UP PADDLE

➡ *learn how to paddleboard in 15 minutes*

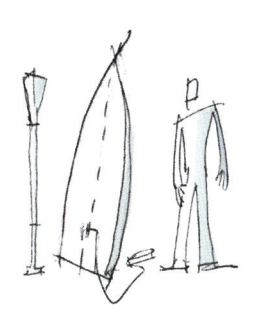

**ROD JONSHON**

*Preamble*

paddleboarding is not so challenging, however there are some mistakes that you should absolutely avoid

you may have witnessed some tragicomical performance on the beach, during which protagonist on duty entertained the swimmers trying for half an hour and in every way to stand on the board (stand-up precisely) ...without however succeeding at all!

so, if you don't want to be the protagonist of the next beach show, here's how you can proceed...

Copyright © 2020
contact: *dotimage@fastwebnet.it*

**Edition I - 2020 (EN)**

**ISBN: 9798582913634**

*All rights reserved.
This book or any portion thereof
may not be reproduced or used in any
manner whatsoever without express
written permission of the publisher.*

# SIZE (1)
## [ choose the board ]

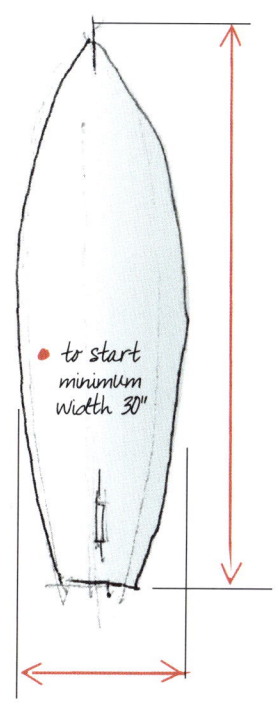

> To start, choose a board of adequate size, essentially the larger it is the easier it will be to maintain balance
>
> choose the board according to your weight:
>
> **< 130 lbs → 200 liters**
> **130-180 lbs → 240 liters**
> **> 180 lbs → 300 liters**

- to start minimum width 30"

– depending on your skill level, you can then opt for a less voluminous or narrower board and therefore faster but less stable

– see pages 32-33

### length
expressed in feet

A long board is more directional and faster than a short board which is slower and more maneuverable

**touring / race / trekking:** from 12 feet up
**allround:** 10 to 12 feet
**surf / river:** less than 10 feet

### width
expressed in inches

A wide board is more stable than a narrow board

a narrow board is less stable but faster

**river:** 30 to 36 inches
**trekking / touring / allround:** 28 to 32 inches
**surf:** 25 to 30 inches
**race:** the tighter it is... the faster it is

### volume
expressed in liters

> Thickness of the board together with width and length defines the volume of a board

the larger the volume, the more the board will float and the more stable it will be, but you will have less handling and responsiveness

the smaller the volume, the more manageable and responsive the board will be, but you will have less stability

3

## ● personal paddle length

Adjust the length of the paddle before boarding. Length is proportional to your build and corresponds approximately to your height + 6"

wider board = longer paddle ✱
Surf/River (shorter) = height + 4"
Race/Touring (longer) = height + 8"

[shaka]

clip

- paddle in 2 pieces, adjustable by loosening the clip

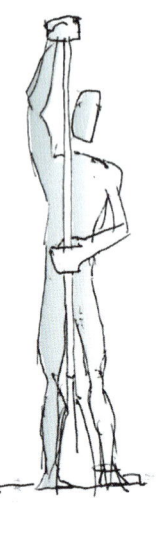

## method 1

place the paddle vertically in front of you, stretch one arm upwards and adjust the length so that you can hold the T-grip with the wrist bent at 90°

✱ consider that several elements affect the paddle adjustment such as width and thickness of the board and the activity you intend to perform

— see page 32

## (2) PADDLE
[ how to size ]

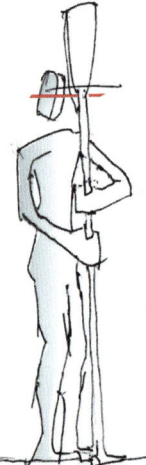

## method 2

lay the paddle upside down in contact with the ground and adjust the length

the junction point between the shaft and the blade should be at eye level

# TERMS 3
[ paddlers slang... ]

## board

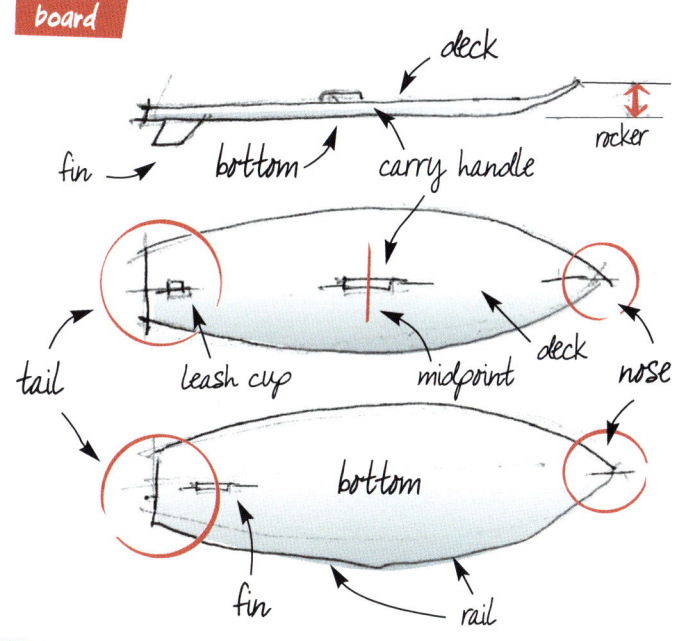

- deck
- rocker
- fin
- bottom
- carry handle
- tail
- leash cup
- midpoint
- deck
- nose
- bottom
- fin
- rail

## paddle

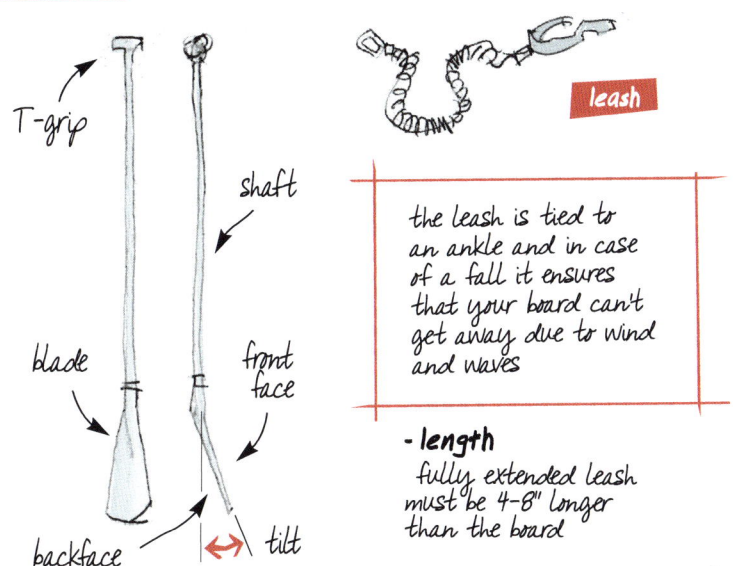

- T-grip
- shaft
- blade
- front face
- backface
- tilt

## leash

the leash is tied to an ankle and in case of a fall it ensures that your board can't get away due to wind and waves

### - length
fully extended leash must be 4-8" longer than the board

5

# 1 boarding

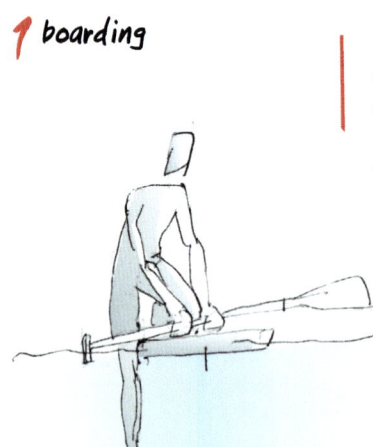

Prevent the board from tilting by placing your hands and knees near the centreline

[centreline]

## at the beach

move away from the shoreline until the water level reaches your knees

- before getting on the board fasten the leash to your ankle

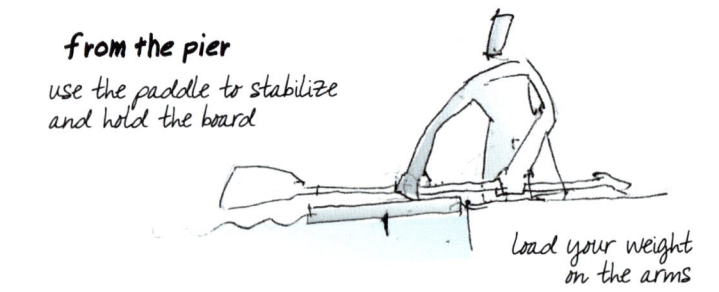

## from the pier

use the paddle to stabilize and hold the board

load your weight on the arms

place your knees symmetrically on the board, on the sides of carry handle

- place your hand and knee beyond the centreline

Finally, check that the setup is correct, the board must not be inclined

# How to start?

the paddle should be held below the T-grip

**2** initially you paddle sitting on your heels, the low center of gravity increases stability

**3** after a few meters you can get up on your knees, paddling becomes more effective and you become familiar with the attitude of the board

- Practice for a few minutes, learn to control your direction, a path of a hundred meters is useful to assimilate the movements and get used to the balance

paddle on one side and then the other to understand the effects of paddling

if you paddle from one side the board will head to the opposite side, to proceed in a straight line you will have to alternate the working side every 5-10 strokes

# STAND UP (5)
[ upright! ]

- Place both hands on the board and place your feet where your knees were, beside the carry handle [midpoint]

balance your weight on feet and then stand up slowly, to maintain your balance better, look ahead and keep your back straight

place the paddle in front of you, in the center of the board

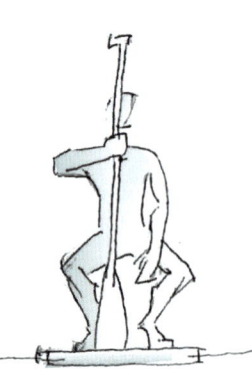

while straightening your legs slide your hands on the paddle, if you are in trouble you can also use it as a third point of support

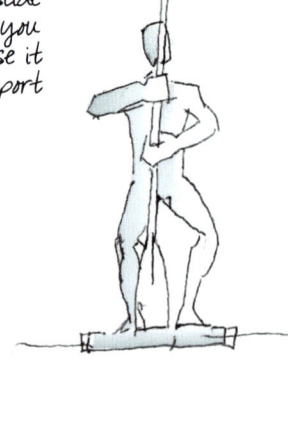

- once you have reached an upright position, use the paddle as a support and maintain the position, keep your knees slightly bent

  - relax and get familiar with the buoyancy

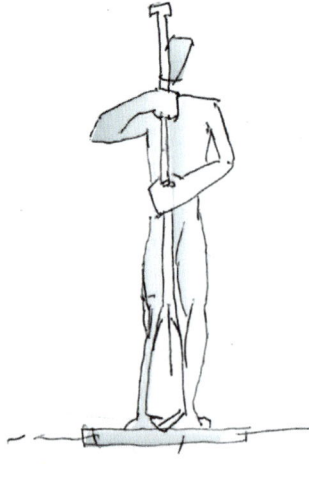

## ✳ hold the paddle

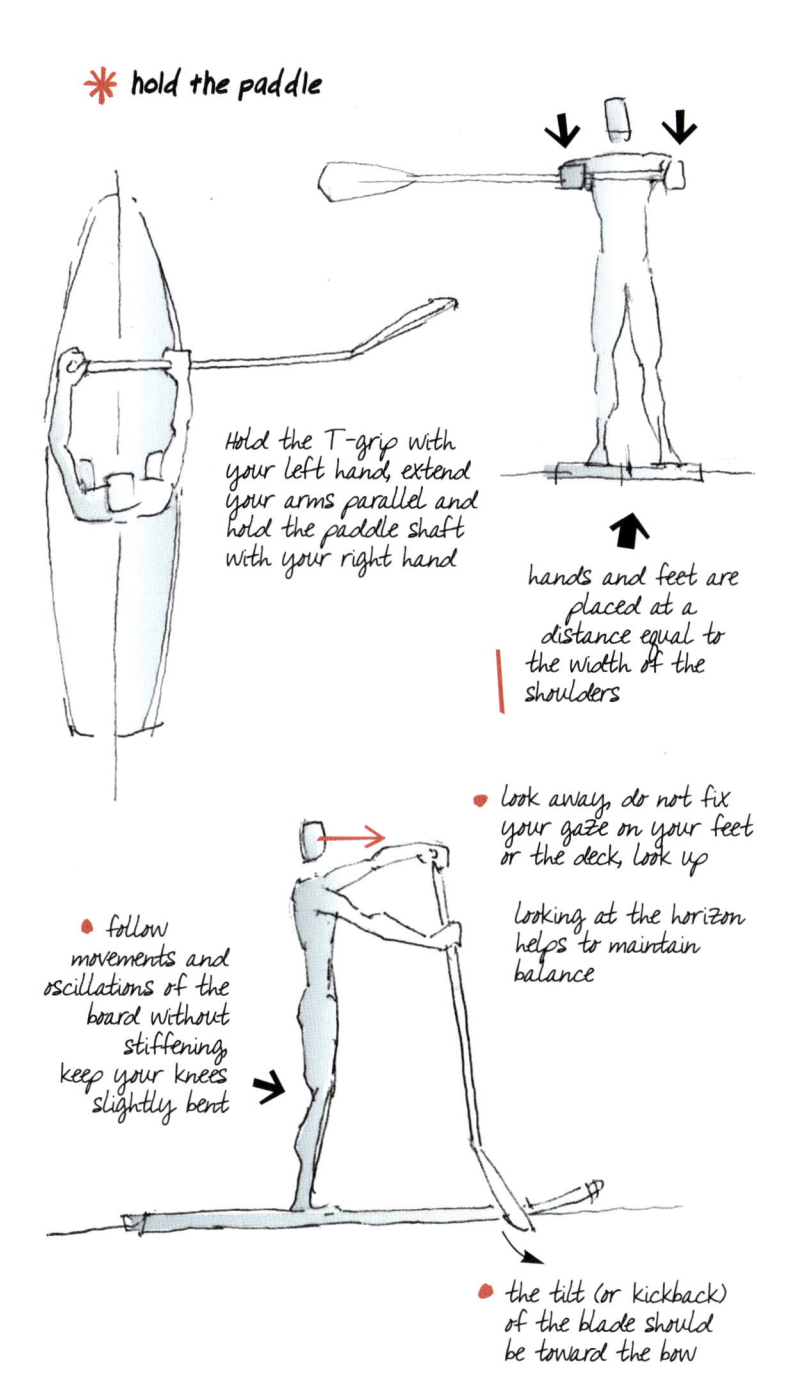

Hold the T-grip with your left hand, extend your arms parallel and hold the paddle shaft with your right hand

hands and feet are placed at a distance equal to the width of the shoulders

- follow movements and oscillations of the board without stiffening, keep your knees slightly bent

- look away, do not fix your gaze on your feet or the deck, look up

looking at the horizon helps to maintain balance

- the tilt (or kickback) of the blade should be toward the bow

9

⊕ Lakes [flatwater] are a perfect environment to take your "first steps" on the paddleboard. The reduced presence of waves also allows the use of Race boards, wich are better-performing but less suitable for wave use because they are long and narrow

Activity on flatwater is similar to the various disciplines of long-distance running, and requires training, perseverance and technique refinement to make the rhythm and power of paddling more effective

# PADDLING (6)
[ forward stroke ]

~~Moving the water~~
the goal of effective paddling is to move the board, not move the water!

● **catch**

slightly flex the upper arm and extend the lower arm to bring the paddle to the bow

focus on the catch phase, dip the blade and start applying force on the paddle

extend your upper arm, your hand pushes forward towards the bow

● **power**

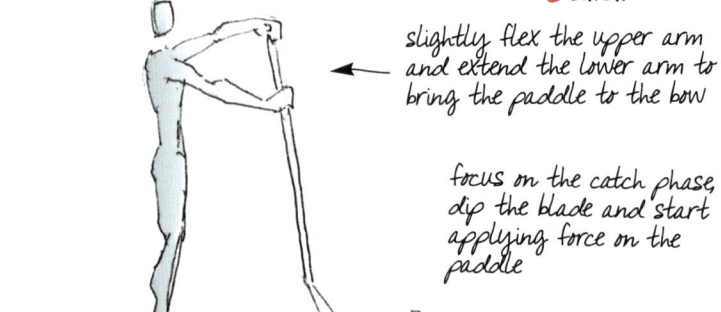

be progressive and adapt stroke pace to the speed you want to maintain

apply a constant force, without accelerating the motion

pulling too hard or too short does not result in effective propulsion

keep your upper arm extended

| Paddling is a composite movement: arms / shoulders / slight upper body rotation

in the final phase rotate the shoulders slightly and use the dorsal muscles

● **release**

when the hand is at your thigh

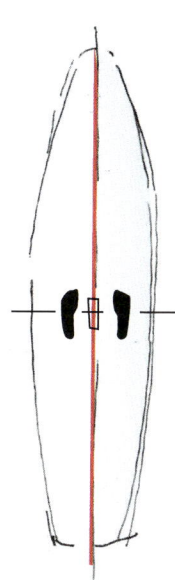

### • recovery and aerial phase

> a correct release does not raise splashes or water, in the aerial phase you reach the bow with the paddle, the blade moves close to the surface of the water, without touching it

• When paddling keep your feet parallel and aligned, a position with feet apart or asymmetrical reduces the stability and control
  - also spacing the feet too far apart is not useful, instead of increasing stability it reduces it

## straight and parallel stroke

forward stroke must be straight and parallel to the rail of board,
an arching stroke increases the turn effect

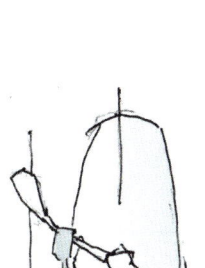

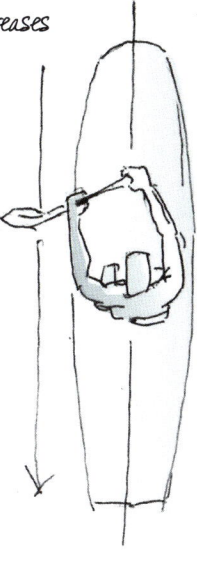

• to properly paddle imagine the paddle is at a stationary point on the water:
it is the board that moves not the paddle

# 7/ PADDLE CHANGE
[ switch sides ]

Make the change quickly to avoid losing speed

position the hand that was on the T-grip below the hand on the shaft...

...move the paddle to the other side and start the next stroke

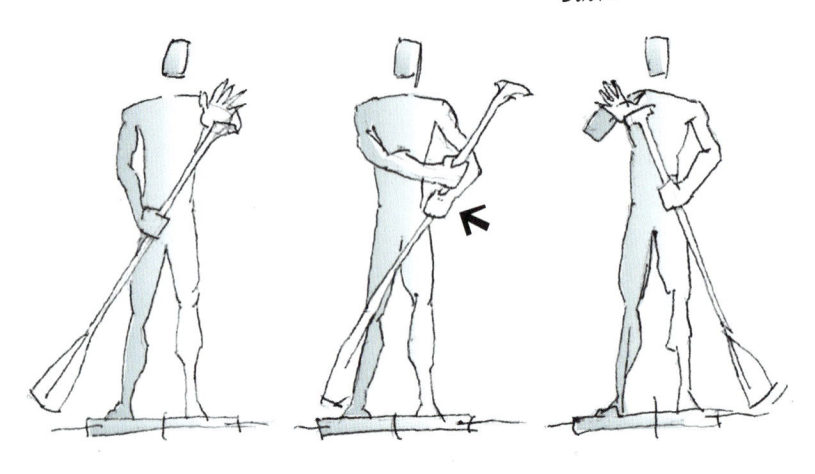

- each stroke causes a slight deviation to the opposite side, the paddleboard travels a slightly curved path, to proceed in a straight line you must alternate the working side every 10-15 strokes

### Side swing

try to swing the board by shifting (gently) your weight on your feet, this exercise improves balance

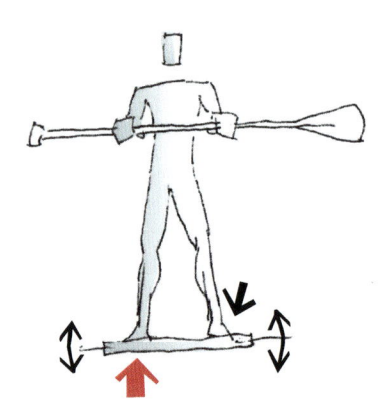

— performs this maneuver while stopped

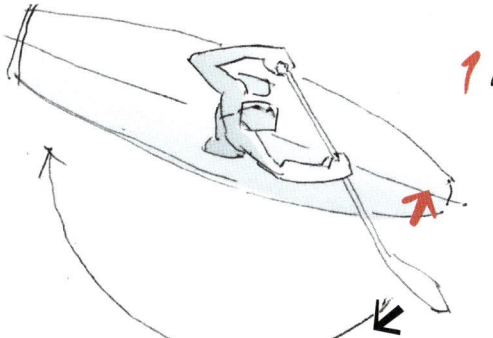

# 8) HOW TO TURN
### [ sweep stroke ]

**1** place the paddle very close to the nose of the board

**2** make an arching movement, the paddle must follow a semicircle,

wider motion gives more pronounced turn action

- the board must turn with no or very little forward movement

in the propulsion stroke you try to make the strokes as straight as possible, but when you want to change direction you have to make the stroke as arched as possible

- bend your knees to increase paddling radius

- shoulders follow the paddle movement

**3** complete the stroke reaching tail

15

# 9 REVERSE TURN

[ reverse sweep stroke ]

**1** start paddling near the tail, pushing the paddle out and forward

**2** as in the sweep stroke the paddle must follow an arc, the wider the arching motion, the more effective the maneuver

- keep your knees bent to increase paddling radius

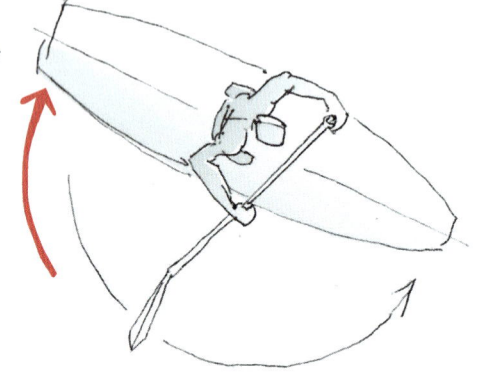

**3** follow through until you reach the nose

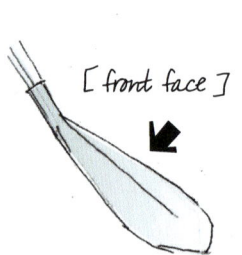

[ front face ]

in the back-strokes you work on front face of the blade, it's <u>not</u> necessary to rotate the paddle

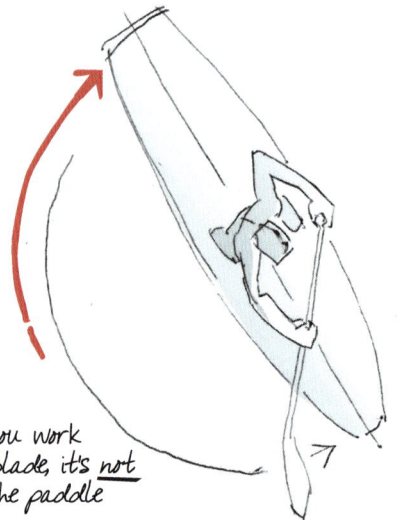

# (10) REVERSE STROKE
### [ or stop stroke ]

back strokes are used when it is necessary to proceed backwards or to slow down / stop when you are in motion

the work of the arms is inverted the lower arm in push, the upper one in pull

the stroke is straight and parallel to the rail, if the paddle goes through an arc it increases the turning effect

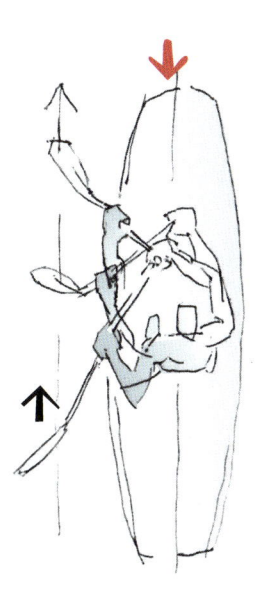

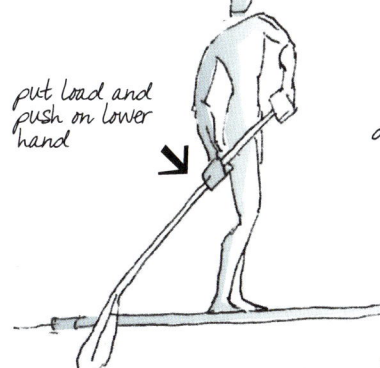

# (11) STEERING
### [ rudder stroke ]

it's used to make a change of direction when you are in motion, with an effect similar to the rudder of a boat

put load and push on lower hand

the purpose of this maneuver is to rotate the board and *not* to slow it down

an effective rudder stroke will result in minimal speed reduction

the amplitude of movement is limited excessive load slows down you without increasing turning action

*the* ③ *elements*

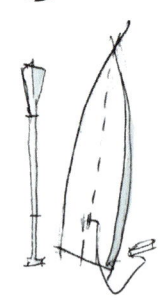

balance is the key to good SUPing, as it allows you to better deal with maneuvers, waves and tricks. Improve your balance and you will reduce your fatigue

# 1 BALANCE

# 2 QUICKNESS

in maneuvering, surfing and trouble conditions you can't hesitate,

acting fast is not synonymous with acting hastily

if you are looking for speed learn to paddle quickly ;)

# 3 POWER

as in any sport that takes place in water even on the paddleboard brute force is not profitable

water is a liquid and not a solid, you must therefore be fluid and never abrupt, sinking the paddle too much is useless,
applying too much traction to the paddle is counterproductive

# 🚫 DownWind
[ ride the waves ]

moving with favorable wind and waves, this condition allows us to reduce the muscular effort and to reach a higher speed
In ideal conditions, and with proper skill, it's possible to cover considerable distances riding on a single wave, or surfing the waves that form along the way, one after the other

⊕ Sea trips [touring] are certainly among the most rewarding activities, even in short excursions you must always remember safety (lifejacket, leash, drybag with cell phone and a minimum reserve of water)

06/2017

# (12) J-STROKE
### [ the hook ]

This movement serves to reduce the deviation towards the opposite side to the working one

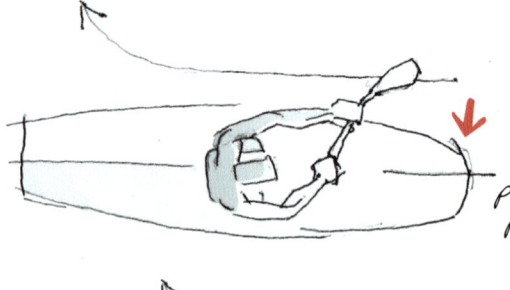

- **catch**

in the J stroke the phases of catch and power are the same as the standard paddling

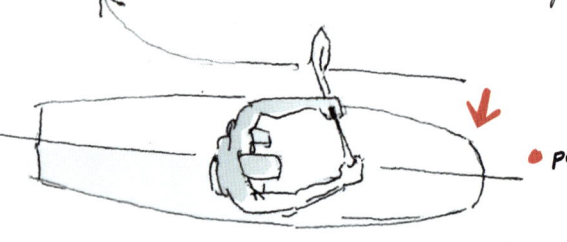

- **power**

- the rotation movement is performed with the wrists of both hands

*paddle rotation 90°*

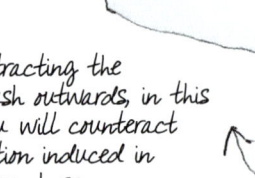

while extracting the blade push outwards, in this way you will counteract the rotation induced in the power phase

- **release**

- **aerial phase**

make the reach with the blade in the cut (remember that if the paddle touches the water, movement is slowed down)

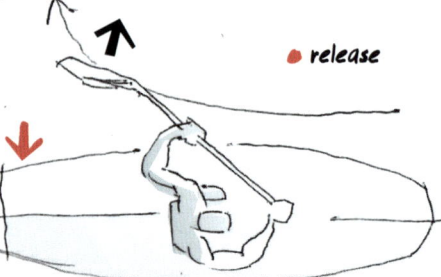

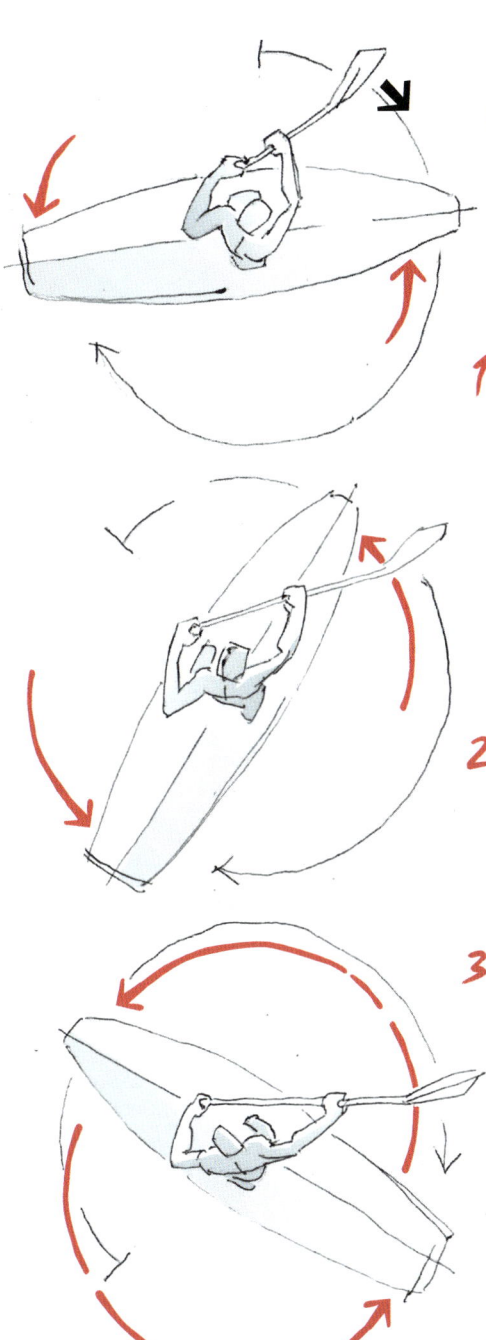

# EXTENDED SWEEP STROKE
## [ crossbow turn ]   (13)

This maneuver involves a cross-draw stroke (using the paddle on the opposite side without changing hands)

**1** dive the paddle on the opposite side, rotate the shoulders and twist your body to bring paddle as far as possible

perform the first part of the movement, pull the paddle out and pass over the bow

**2** as in the standard sweep stroke, the paddle draws an arc, the wider the semicircle the more effective the maneuver will be

**3** complete the paddle up to the stern

---

bring your hands closer together to increase the paddle working radius

narrower handle = wider radius

21

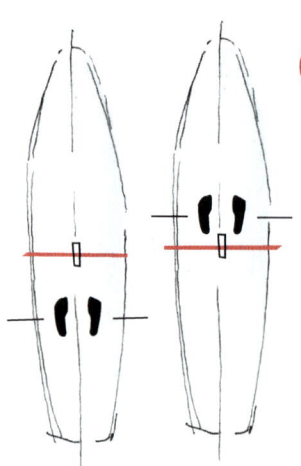

## (14) LENGTHWISE STANCE

Moving your foothold changes the behavior of the board

- **back**: it is easier to change direction, you reduce the board directional properties (maneuvers / surf / waves)

- **forward**: the board is more directional and less maneuverable (flatwater / touring)

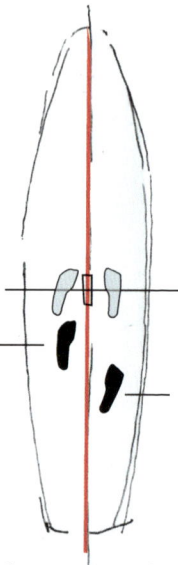

[ step back ]

### ✳ SEQUENCE

- move your left foot slightly toward the center of the board with a slight rotation

- shift your body weight to your left foot

- the right foot (working side) is thus relieved of weight and can be moved one step back (towards the tail)

shifting load of one foot to the back of the board increases the handling, this position also allows you to use the paddle over the tail

you can just move one foot or place both feet towards the stern.

## 15 STEPBACK TURN
[ pivot turn heelside ]

**1** move to the back of board [step back] until the nose rises out of the water

**2** twist your body and shoulders to bring the paddle over the tail

**3** continue the movement as in the reverse sweep stroke, the paddle must follow an arc, the wider the motion the more effective the maneuver will be

- bend your knees to lower your centre of gravity and bring your hands closer together to increase the paddle working radius

**4** push the paddle forward and complete the stroke to the nose

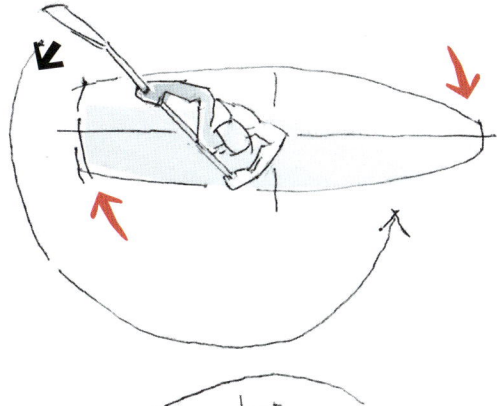

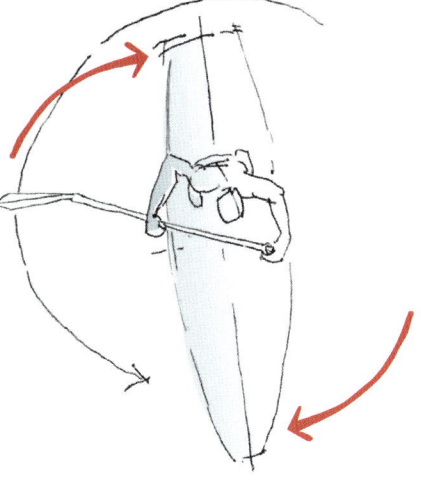

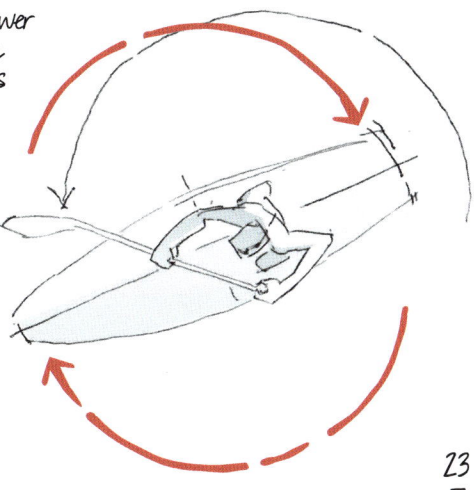

23

# 🟥 RIVER

current is the reference element in river practice, the equivalent of wind and waves at sea

| carefully evaluate the intensity of the current, possible landing points and possible obstacles

in a placid, slow-moving river, the current can reach 4-5 km/h, a speed that is already sufficient to make going upstream ineffective and very tiring.

| if the force of the current exceeds your capabilities, do not attempt to move upstream

- to cross a watercourse don't waste energy trying to fight the current, paddle on the downstream side and point towards the shore, you will land on the opposite side further downstream

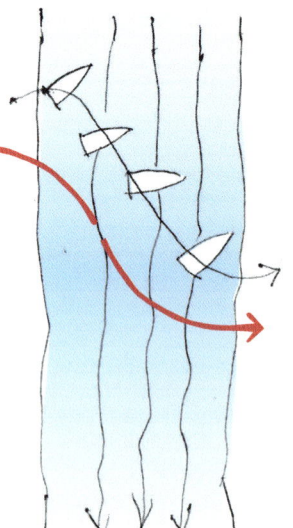

[ ferry ]

(!) Branches and artificial obstacles on the river are an inconspicuous but serious hazard. Stay away!

## ✳ JUMP START

to make the flatwater experience more dynamic, you can place the board in the water and after a run-up (more or less short...) jump on the board, in this way you will obtain a 15-30 feet long glide

⊕ On rivers and streams [River/Whitewater] polyethylene boards without drifts are used, adapted to the particular conditions of use (impacts, friction on obstacles). A leash is not used, which in flowing water could represent an element of risk instead of safety

## 16 FALL

If you lose your balance, don't try to recover by clinging to the board, you risk falling on it

push off with a dive

push the paddle away from your body without releasing grip

← hold the paddle

push the board away with your feet

## ↑ HOW TO REMOUNT

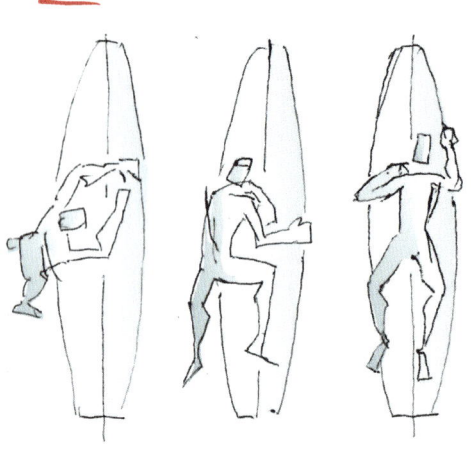

### • from the side

while got the middle of the board [midpoint] pull your upper body onto the board, then put one leg on it towards the tail

> do not try to get back on the board by lifting yourself up on the arms

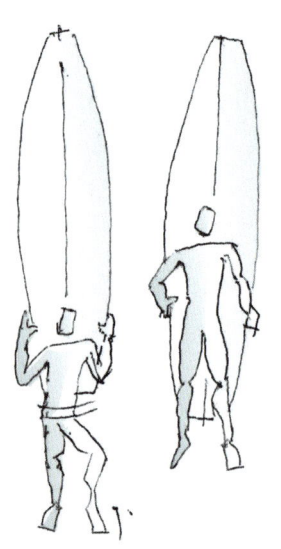

### • getting back at the tail

place your hands on the tail and put your weight on to sink the board

with both hands grab the edges of the board

put your upper body on the board, you can kick your feet to help pull your whole body onto the board

lying in a prone position move to the midline

26

# !! SAFETY

Safety is a boring subject, let's face it...
When we're SUPing we'd like to think only of the fun!
But think about it, whether you're in the sea, on a lake or on a river, you're on the water... and an event that on land is harmless and trivial on the water can easily turn into a challenging and risky situation

## WEATHER

If you plan to move away from the coast or go on an excursion of a few hours, always check the situation and the weather forecast, as wind and waves can make the return trip more challenging than expected
On streams, heavy rainfall can also be a risk factor

## Lifejacket / PFD

[personal flotation device]
Wear or take with you if you intend to move away from beach areas, when the water and air temperatures are low, and in all those situations where getting back on the board can be difficult
[may be required to wear a PFD when paddling outside of swim and surf areas]

(!) Required equipment and allowed distance from the coast may vary - check local rules

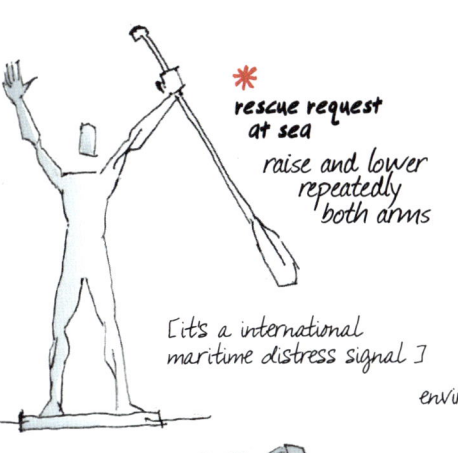

### * rescue request at sea

raise and lower repeatedly both arms

[it's a international maritime distress signal]

if you are tired or environmental conditions make it necessary, switch to a kneeling position

you can also lie on the board with the paddle under you and swim with your arms (synchronous or alternating)

**leash + dry bag + water**

# SURF
[ waves... ]

Waves are a changing and dynamic phenomenon, understanding and predicting their behavior is a skill that is acquired only with time ...spent between waves

**1** start on small waves lying in prone position to acquire the necessary sensitivity

**2** switch to standing position shift your weight forward and use the paddle to increase speed and stay on the wave

**3** try larger waves, standing upright (with even feet or in surf-stance)

**4** finally, if the wave is high enough and if you are fast enough, the board will go into surf... it's done!

> to practice, choose an area free of obstacles and with few people - keep a distance from other surfers

## SURF STANCE
[ californian style... ]

- improves side balance
- greater control of the bow/stern load, allows to getting wave more easily

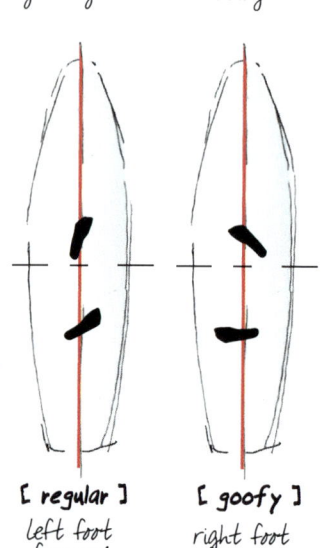

[ regular ]
left foot forward

[ goofy ]
right foot forward

## 17 BRACE STROKE
[ balance support ]

this movement allows you to maintain or restore balance, if you are stationary you will have to move the paddle forward

paddle parallel to the water

while moving, simply slide the paddle on the surface of the water

- the paddle blade works almost parallel to the surface and slides without sinking

⊕ Waves!! SUPing offers some advantages over the wave funboards, standing you have a better view of the wave than lying down, there is no need to learn the movement to stand up [take off], you can surf smaller waves and you can do cruising, that is to move in the "spot" to wait for the wave more suitable, finally the paddle offers the advantage of a third point of support

# WHITEWATER
[ stream ]

this term indicates a watercourse with a rating between class IV and class VI

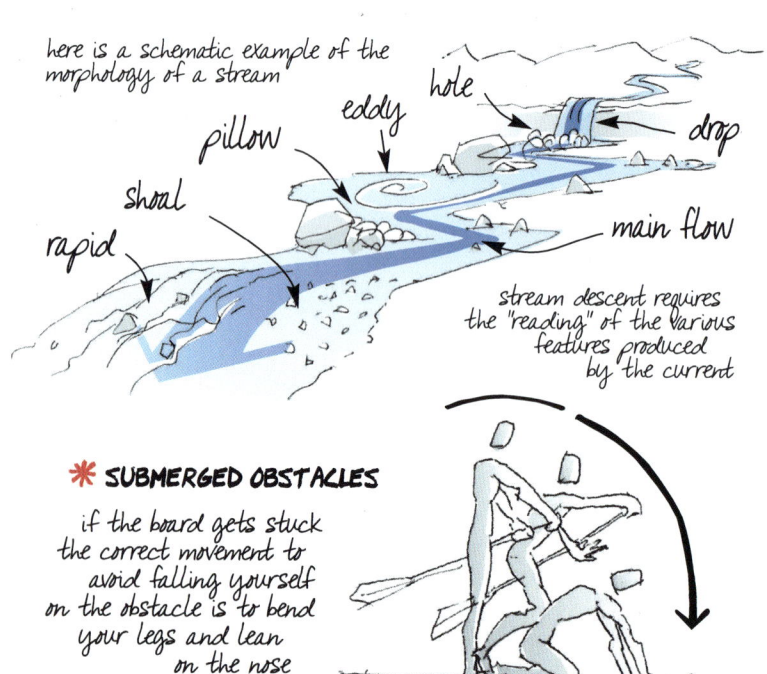

here is a schematic example of the morphology of a stream

- hole
- eddy
- pillow
- drop
- shoal
- main flow
- rapid

stream descent requires the "reading" of the various features produced by the current

## ✳ SUBMERGED OBSTACLES

if the board gets stuck the correct movement to avoid falling yourself on the obstacle is to bend your legs and lean on the nose

## (18) DRAW STROKE
[ sideways move ]

this movement allows you to move laterally without the board turning

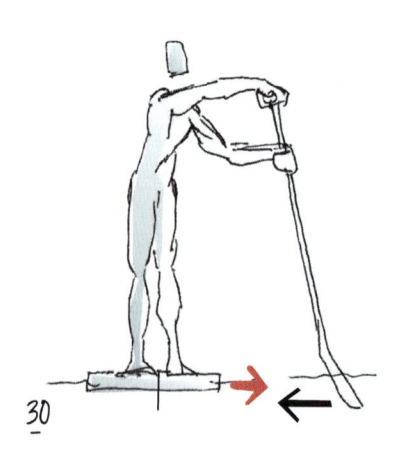

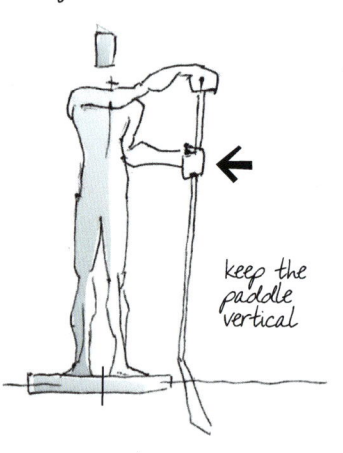

keep the paddle vertical

⊕ Down-river running [whitewater] is not a practice that can be improvised, it is advisable to start with a descent accompanied by an instructor or attend a dedicated course.

(!) Always wear lifejacket + helmet

# 19 Equipment
[ boards & paddles ]

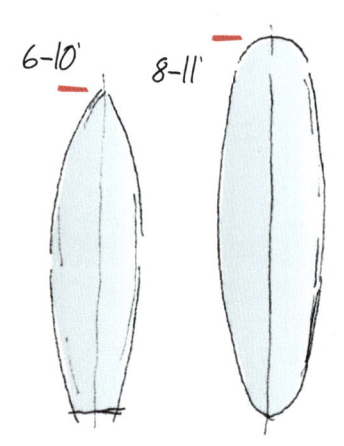

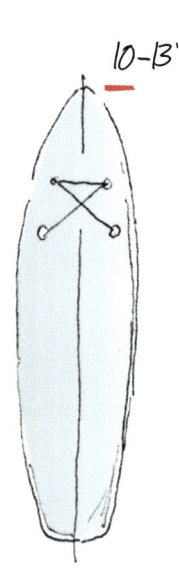

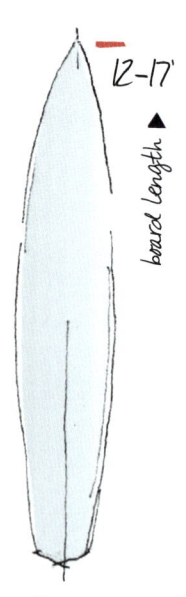

6-10'  8-11'  10-13'  12-17'

board length ▶

## SURF
short, reduced thickness, a more pronounced rocker (nose curve), flat bottom (planing), up to 3 fins

Minimum volume liters = body weight x 2

## ALLROUND
polyvalent, they represent a compromise between stability, maneuverability and speed
- also suitable for whitewater use

## TOURING
[ longboard ]

stable and quite fast, ideal for long duration exits

- sea
- flatwater

## RACE
very smooth, light and narrow, pointed bow and tail, the hull can be V-shaped (displacement), the lightest are made of composite / carbon fiber

thruster set-up

## PADDLE — see pages 3-4
**fixed:** lighter and stiffer (not adjustable)
**adjustable:** (in 2-3 parts) easier to transport, can also be taken apart

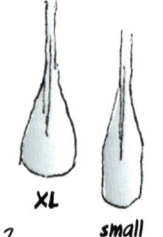

the blade size is a choice that depends on your strength and the discipline you practice.

| larger: more power in maneuvers but more difficult to maintain a high paddling cadence

| smaller: reduced capacity for acceleration, less effort in controlling the paddle, higher cadence

**XL**  **small**

32

|     **+**<br>pros | **−**<br>cons |
|---|---|

## Rigid
**EPS foam + Fiberglass / Carbon fiber + epoxy / PU resin**
**HD - Polyethylene**

| | |
|---|---|
| • higher performance, faster and smoother — the hull can have a sharper design<br>• greater reactivity in maneuvers<br>• no bending in the waves — surf more easily | • most delicate, suffers shocks and chafing<br>• greater bulk in transport and storage<br>• more harmful in case of fall/impact on the body |

## Inflatable
**PVC / pressure 12 - 25 psi**

| | |
|---|---|
| • transport is much easier, when the board is deflated it takes up less space<br>• it does not suffer from impacts against obstacles in the water and on land | − the bending of the hull dissipates part of the paddling energy<br>• with the same length, lower top speed (about 10%)<br>• less reactivity in maneuvers<br>• possible puncture on sharp objects |

# 20 Clothing

In ideal conditions SUPing is practiced in swimsuit and does not require specific clothing

on the water you are fully exposed to sun radiation, you can use a sunscreen (waterproof) or a Lycra T-shirt to protect you from UV rays

### 100° rule

if the sum of the water and air temperatures is greater than 100°F you are not at risk of hypothermia,
below this value it is necessary to wear thermal clothing

• for surfing you can use a neoprene wetsuit (short or long)
 − if you have to paddle for a long time, a combination that does not hinder movement is more suitable:
  • neoprene shorts + paddling jacket
   − for colder temperatures:
• neoprene bib and socks + long sleeve paddling jacket

I hope what I have explained on these pages has helped you, for all the rest all you need is

...practice, practice and more practice
(and a bit of technique too)

Enjoy! :)

Northern Paddlers Association

Printed in Great Britain
by Amazon